Ethics

Behave Yourself!

Ethics (Behave Yourself!)
First Edition published by Enable Training and Consulting, Inc.
Three Hundred and Ten Main Street East, Milton, Ont.

The author acknowledges the generous assistance of the Ontario Arts Council in the form of a Writer's Reserve grant.

ONTARIO ARTS COUNCIL
CONSEIL DES ARTS DE L'ONTARIO

International Standard Book Number: 978-0-9868681-3-9

Author: Amy Leask
Design and Illustration: Mark Hughes
Additional Illustration: Ami Moore
Editor, Publisher: Ben Zimmer

Printed in Canada

Enable Training and Consulting
310 Main St. E., Unit 104
Milton, Ont., Canada L9T 1P4
905.864.1858
1.877.872.4619
www.enabletc.com
www.kidsthinkaboutit.com

etc
ENABLE TRAINING & CONSULTING, INC.

Let your beautiful brain bubble and brew with bright ideas! Massage your magnanimous mind with multitudes of musings! Quip, query, and question! Wander through the weird and wonderful world of Why!

Do you ever wonder:

- What it means to be a good person?
- How to tell the difference between right and wrong?
- If it's ever okay to be a little bit selfish?
- How to do the right thing for many people at the same time?
- Whether everyone should have to follow the same rules?

If you do, you are like me, Sophia the Wise. You are a philosopher! Philosophers are people who ask big questions- the biggest questions possible. They also try to find answers to these questions- and there are a lot of answers, very cool ones.

Let the thinking begin!

IN THIS ISSUE!

Talk about people who have the "right" stuff! These great minds will get you thinking about living the good life!

Full Name: John Stuart Mill
Born: 1806 AD
Died: 1873 AD
Hometown: London, England
Fave Subjects: How To Be Good, Power, How To Make A Good Argument
Career Highlights: was from a family of famous thinkers, learned to speak Greek at the age of 3, worked with his wife to defend the rights of women, was a member of British Parliament

Full Name: Epicurus
Born: 341 BC
Died: 270 BC
Hometown: Samos, Greece
Fave Subjects: How To Be Good, Science, The Nature Of The Universe
Career Highlights: created his own school of philosophy called "The Garden", one of the first thinkers to talk about how science should be done, influenced how democracy and government worked, even hundreds of years later

Full Name: Alisa Zinov'yevna Rosenbaum (later Ayn Rand)
Born: 1905 AD
Died: 1982 AD
Hometown: Saint Petersburg, Russia
Fave Subjects: How To Be Good, Power, Minds And Bodies, Truth, Knowledge And Understanding, Beauty And Art
Career Highlights: worked as a writer in the movie industry, wrote novels, plays and movie scripts, along with philosophy books, published her own magazines

Full Name: Immanuel Kant
Born: 1724 AD
Died: 1804 AD
Hometown: Konigsberg, Prussia (now Kaliningrad, Russia)
Fave Subjects: How To Be Good, Truth, Knowledge And Understanding, Beauty And Art, Power, Astronomy
Career Highlights: won an award for making a discovery about the way Earth rotates, did most of his important work in philosophy after the age of 50, wrote more than 30 books on philosophy and other subjects

Full Name: Simone Ernestine Lucie Marie Bertrand de Beauvoir
Born: 1908 AD
Died: 1986 AD
Hometown: Paris, France
Fave Subjects: How To Be Good, Freedom, Power
Career Highlights: was the youngest person ever to pass the *agrégation* exam in France, wrote novels, short stories, essays, philosophy, and travel stories, fought hard for women to be treated as equals, had a bridge named after her in Paris

I can't tell you how many times I've been told to be good.
"Be good, Sophia! Don't stuff beans up your nose!"
"Be good, Sophia! Don't use the goldfish as finger puppets!"
"Be good, Sophia! Don't paint a mustache on Grandma while she's sleeping!"

Sheesh! Have you ever wondered why it's such a good thing to be good? Wouldn't it be better if we could do whatever we wanted, whenever we wanted, without having to worry about being good?

What would the world be like without any rules? If we were allowed to do whatever we wanted, we could let our rooms get so messy that they started to stink like an elephant's behind. We could sneak bites of someone else's pizza while they weren't looking, and ride any bike we wanted. We could play silly tricks on people, like putting gum in their comic books, and it would be okay.

But there would be one very big problem. If we were allowed to do whatever we wanted, then no one else would have to behave themselves either. They could steal all our stuff and call us names. They could poke us with sticks and secretly tie our shoelaces together while we were eating lunch. If we were allowed to do whatever we wanted, so could everyone else, and we probably wouldn't want that.

So how do we figure out what being good really means? How do we know which rules to follow? Philosophers have a lot of different ideas about this.

Idea One: MAKE SOME RULES AND STICK TO THEM!

Some philosophers think it's all about making rules that everyone can follow, all of the time. For example, some people say we should always be polite. Some people say we should never steal things. Some people say we should never hurt other people. These rules, if they're good ones, could be used by anyone, at any time, in any situation.

Sometimes things get difficult, and we have to choose between two important rules, or three, or four. We might have rules about always telling the truth, and we might have rules about never hurting anyone's feelings, but sometimes we have to hurt people's feelings in order to tell the truth.

If you could make rules for everyone to follow all of the time, what would they be? It might be a long, long list!

Idea Two MAKE EVERYONE HAPPY!

Some philosophers think we should try to make as many people as happy as possible. Instead of one person eating an entire chocolate cake, it's better to have twelve people each eating a slice. Instead of one person listening to a song, it's better to have many people listening.

A lot of the time, this means changing the rules for every new situation. What makes people happy at one time may be very different at another, and it's almost impossible to make everyone happy at once. People are strange that way. What could you do to make a lot of people happy at the same time? Wow, that's a tricky one!

Idea Three MAKE YOURSELF A BETTER PERSON!

There are other philosophers who think we should do things that make us better people. We should do things that teach us to be more generous, fair, polite, or calm. When we share our lunch with a friend, we learn to be generous. When we teach our little sister to catch frogs, we learn to be patient. Being good is like exercising. If we play lots of sports, and do lots of work, we might grow big, bulgy muscles. If we're good, we could grow stronger in our hearts and in our minds. Which new and improved qualities would you like to have?

Idea Four BE SELFISH!

A few philosophers even think it's okay to be selfish sometimes. This doesn't mean we can't be polite to other people too, just that we're not mean to ourselves. We can lend library books to our friends, but only if we have finished reading them first. We can listen to our parents and clean our rooms, but only if it makes us feel better too. A lot of people might feel funny about being selfish, but it's still nice to make ourselves feel... nice. How would making yourself happy affect other people? Ah, to be a little selfish... Sophia the Wise should sometimes be the most important person.

So far, no one's really figured out what being good is all about. Luckily, I've found a whole bunch of famous philosophers who can help us get a jump on this question.

Meet Mr. Epicurus (Ep-ick-yur-us)

Sophia: Let's take a little jaunt to Greece to meet our first thinker, who was cooking up big questions more than two thousand, three hundred years ago. Way back then, the sun would shine over the Parthenon (a pretty impressive building), soft breezes would blow over the Aegean sea, and Mr. Epicurus would come up with some pretty spiffy ideas.

Mr. Epicurus: Good to meet you, Sophia. I liked talking about philosophy so much that I made a school for it at my house, in my garden. My students and I spent a lot of time there, trying to figure out how to live a good life.

Sophia: Beautiful thoughts amongst the beautiful flowers! I love it! While you were listening to the birds sing and the bugs hum, what did you figure out?

Mr. Epicurus: It's funny you should ask that, Sophia. A garden is a place of pleasure. It makes us feel good. It's no wonder that my students and I decided that the right thing to do with our lives was to always try to feel good.

Sophia: Wahooo! I can get on board with feeling good! I like to stay in my pajamas all day long, and eat cookie dough, and watch cartoons…

Mr. Epicurus: Hold on there, Sophia! Doing the right thing isn't quite that simple. Feeling good doesn't always mean doing whatever you feel like doing.

Sophia: Bah! I was afraid you'd say that.

Mr. Epicurus: Tell me Sophia, what would happen if you watched cartoons all day in your pajamas, and you ate nothing but cookie dough, and then all of the sudden, you weren't allowed to do that anymore? Would those things still make you feel good?

Sophia: I'd miss all of those things terribly, of course. I'd probably be more miserable than I was before I had them. I might even wish that I'd never tasted cookie dough…

Mr. Epicurus: Let's not get too carried away, Sophia. It's natural to want to eat, and to be comfortable. What my students and I thought was that happiness and pleasure could be found in living a simple life, in which we got what we really needed, and learned not to wish for too many fancy things. Making the right choices means being satisfied with getting just enough food and water to keep us healthy, and a good education to build healthy minds. All the little "extras" in life, like cookie dough, are lovely, but we shouldn't get too hung up on them.

Sophia: Doing the right thing means doing simple things, even without cookie dough and my pajamas. I think I could get used to that!

Meet Mr. Kant (Can't)

Sophia: And now, presenting a stupendous brain from Germany! Mr. Kant lived about two hundred fifty years ago, and he had some very interesting things to say about being good.

Mr. Kant: How very kind of you to ask me here, Sophia. I lived and worked my whole life in the same town. It was a wonderful place, full of great thinkers who liked to share ideas.

Sophia: Tell us a bit about your life, Mr. Kant. Were you good all of the time?

Mr. Kant: Goodness me! I don't know if I was good all of the time, but I certainly tried. I actually really loved rules and regulations. When I was a student, I studied very hard and always did my homework. When I was older, I still loved following rules. I got out of bed at exactly the same time every morning. I went for a walk along exactly the same path every day, at exactly the same time. When I went to work, I was never late, and I always did what I needed to do. In every part of my life, I was Mr. Dependable. My neighbors used to set their clocks by my activities! Did you know, Sophia, that I was one of the first people to have a job teaching philosophy at a university?

Sophia: I'll bet your students loved having someone as trusty as you to teach them!

Mr. Kant: I got along just fine with my students. I loved rules so much that I made them part of my philosophy too! I decided that if people were going to be good, there should be rules that everyone should follow, all of the time, in every situation. I didn't think rules about being good should change.

Sophia: That sounds pretty tricky! How do we make rules like that?

Mr. Kant: Believe it or not, I had rules for making rules. Rule number one is that every time you try to be good, imagine what would happen if everyone did the same thing as you. For example, what if everyone threw their trash on the ground?

Sophia: Let's see… we would have sticky shoes, there would be terrible smells, and it would look pretty gross. No sir, trash on the ground is not good.

Mr. Kant: So the rule should be that no one should ever be allowed to throw their trash on the ground. Good people should always put their trash in a garbage can or in a recycling box.

Sophia: Sounds smart. Any other rules?

Mr. Kant: One more. I was also very worried about people doing mean things to each other. I made another rule that even when we're trying to do good things, we should make sure we don't hurt each other. There are lots of other people just like you, and they have feelings just like you do.

Sophia: So if I try to make rules for everyone to follow, and I try my best to look out for other people, then I'm probably being good?

Mr. Kant: It sounds like a very good start. Now, if you'll excuse me, it's time for my walk. I can't be late!

Sophia: You mean, you ***Kant*** be late! (giggle, giggle)

Meet Mr. Mill

Sophia: Some people have doctors in their family. Some people have bakers. Some people have musicians. I'd like you to meet my good friend, Mr. Mill, who came from a family of philosophers in England, almost two hundred years ago. Imagine sitting around the dinner table every night, slurping spaghetti or crunching corn on the cob, and talking about big ideas! Your parents could teach you to play ball and teach you to ask important questions at the same time. You could even discuss the meaning of life on those really long, boring family road trips, instead of flinging cheese puffs at your brother in the back seat. Mr. Mill, can you tell us how to be good?

Mr. Mill: Well, Sophia, while we poured gravy on our mashed potatoes and cut our roast beef into little pieces, my family would talk a lot about how to be good. We talked about how to be good to other people, all kinds of people, and also how to be good to animals. We decided that what people wanted more than anything was to be happy. When I was a little boy, my godfather made a rule: if we really want to be good, we should try to make as many people as happy as possible.

Sophia: That's a simple rule, but it's very interesting. Instead of one person gobbling up an entire

pizza, everyone should have a slice. Instead of one person playing video games by themselves, everyone should have a turn. Instead of one person riding a cool skateboard with racing stripes and purple wheels, everyone should have a chance. When you're trying to decide something important, everyone should get to say what they think.

Mr. Mill: You catch on quickly, Sophia! When I was older, I added my own special idea to this rule. A pizza is great for a while, but it only lasts until you eat the last bite. Video games only last until your parents turn them off, and then it's time to do your homework. Even the coolest skateboard might break or get too small as you grow bigger. These things might make us happy for a little while, but I'm convinced that it's better to find ways to be happy for a long time.

Sophia: Mr. Mill, what kinds of things can make people happy for a long time?

Mr. Mill: Well, having a best friend who shares our love of scary movies can make us happy for a long time. Learning to paint pictures, and studying interesting bugs, and watching stars in the sky (and even going to school) can make us happy for a long time. Helping others to think big ideas can also make us happy for a long time. Happiness is definitely worth thinking about.

Meet Ms. Rand

Sophia: For even more cool thoughts on being good, let's talk to Ms. Rand, a fascinating thinker who was born in Russia, but lived in the United States less than fifty years ago. Take it away, Ms. Rand!

Ms. Rand: What a warm welcome! Tell me, Sophia, would it surprise you to hear that being good can sometimes mean thinking of yourself first?

Sophia: Me first? Little ol' me? Sophia the Wise? I can't wait to hear about this one!

Ms. Rand: This might sound a little strange, but I think most people are a little bit selfish.

Sophia: Shocking! I thought we were supposed to think of other people first!

Ms. Rand: Being a little selfish doesn't mean we should be nasty to other people. It just means that we can do nice things for ourselves too. When I share my lunch with someone, they feel less hungry, but I also feel good because I helped someone. When I hold the door open for someone, they feel happy, but I'm also happy because people think I'm polite.

Sophia: What about when I give my dog a bath? I hate it when he shakes and sprays stinky water all over me. Then I have to chase him all over the house with a towel. Giving my dog a bath doesn't make me very happy. It mostly makes me smelly and soggy. I think I do it just for him, and not for me.

Ms. Rand: Maybe not. It's true that wet dog is a really terrible odor, but even when you're stinky and wet, you still know that you're doing something nice to keep your dog happy and healthy. It may not feel like it right away, but you're doing something for yourself too. Your dog will be your friend for a long time if he's healthy and happy… and he'll be far less smelly when he jumps on your bed and sleeps by your feet.

Sophia: This is true, but I still feel a little weird about being selfish.

Ms. Rand: In my opinion, people can't really help it. Being a little bit selfish is just a part of being human. No matter how hard we try to help other people, we will always be thinking of ourselves at the same time.

Sophia: I think I can live with that. Now I'm going to be a little selfish. I want to learn more philosophy!

Meet Ms. de Beauvoir (duh-bow-voir)

Sophia: *Bonjour*! My last guest is Ms. de Beauvoir, who lived in France less than fifty years ago. Ms. de Beauvoir and her philosopher friends loved to sit outside lovely buildings, look at beautiful gardens, and eat croissants, but most of all, they all loved to think about big ideas. In fact, they had some wonderful arguments, loud enough to shake the Eiffel tower! Ms. de Beauvoir, tell us your views on being good.

Ms. de Beauvoir: *Bien sûr,* Sophia! I was a very determined person when I was young, and I did very well at school. But one day, I looked around and noticed that boys and girls were sometimes expected to do different things. Boys got to read big books, and get big jobs, while girls were supposed to look pretty and be quiet. I realized that I was lucky, and that not all girls got to do all of the same things that I had done.

Sophia: Totally unfair! What did you do?

Ms. de Beauvoir: I realized how important it was for everyone to have freedom to choose the things they want to do. I was given the chance to study, to be a teacher, and to write lots of books. I thought if I could choose all of these wonderful things, then everyone should be able to. In my opinion, the way to be good is to make sure that everyone at least gets a chance to choose what they'd like to be.

Sophia: Hmmmmm…giving everyone the same freedom to do things. I think being good could mean treating people the same even if they're different ages, or if they speak a different language, or if they come from a different place.

Ms. de Beauvoir: *Fantastique, mon amie!* A world where there are many beautiful buildings, many lovely gardens, many croissants, and where all kinds of people are free to choose who they want to be sounds like a really beautiful place, doesn't it?

Sophia: *Oui, oui, mon amie!*

Try It Out: A "Good" Story

Being good is a tricky business, and it might not be as easy as you imagine. Read this story carefully and pick the solution that you think is the best.

Imagine that your class is planning a field trip to an amusement park. All of you will be spending the day on roller coasters that twist and turn in every direction imaginable, but don't make you feel sick. You'll be eating donuts as big as your head, and jumbo hot dogs with blobs of ketchup. You'll be winning teddy bears so gigantic you'll need to borrow a wagon to get them home. The big problem is that the school bus can only hold twenty people, and there are twenty-five people in the class. Worst of all, there is only enough money to pay for one bus.

Hmmmmm ... Would you:

- Cancel the trip? Mr. Kant says we should use the same rules for everyone, and we should always think of other people's feelings. If one person can't go, then maybe no one should go.
- Let most of the people go, but not all of them? Mr. Mill says it's important to make as many people happy as possible, so as long as most of the class can go, then maybe it's okay. We can try to find something fun for the students who stay behind too.
- Jump on the bus! Ms. Rand says it's okay to be selfish sometimes, and you really, really want to go. There will be donuts as big as your head, after all!
- Be happy doing something else that isn't so expensive or complicated? Mr. Epicurus says if we don't get used to having so many fancy things, we won't be disappointed if we can't have them.
- Think about what will give everyone the same chance to choose? Ms. de Beauvoir says we should let everyone have the same freedom.

Formula For Goodness

What makes someone a good person? Read the chart below, and for each characteristic, choose "yes", "no" or "maybe". Don't be afraid to grab a partner and compare ideas. You can also use the extra spaces at the bottom to add more characteristics to the list.

A person is good if...	Yes	No	Maybe
They are honest.			
They are generous.			
They are friendly.			
They are smart.			
They are calm.			
They are fair.			
They are kind.			
They are creative.			
They are brave.			
They are peaceful.			
They are wise.			

What's the worst thing you can do to another person? Why is doing something like this so terrible? What's the best thing you can do for someone? What makes doing this so great? What's the big difference between doing something terrible and doing something wonderful? Use the space below to write or draw your ideas.

Journal Of Thoughts

Name: ______________________________ Date: __________________

BIG WORDS for BIG IDEAS

Philosophy (fill-oss-uff-eee): This means asking giant, weird, interesting questions for which there isn't always an easy answer, but we ask them anyway because they help us to understand ourselves and the universe we live in.

Philosopher (fill-oss-uff-er): This is a very curious person who asks giant, weird, interesting questions. A good philosopher has an open mind, and loves new ideas even more than a good back scratch, their favorite pizza or free toys.

Logic (law-jic): This means thinking clearly. It's a lot harder than it seems. It means not getting upset if someone disagrees with you, and making room for all kinds of ideas, even if you don't like them very much.

Argument: Believe it or not, it's more than just saying the opposite of what someone else says. In philosophy, an argument happens when you say what you think, and then you give a bunch of reasons why you think it. Then, other philosophers tell you if they agree or not, and give their own reasons.

Metaphysics (met-a-fizz-icks) or Theory of Reality: Philosophers just love to think about what is real, and what is imaginary. They also like to think about what the universe is made of, and how time works. Some even like to think about what a human being is made of, and how our minds and bodies work together.

Epistemology (ee-pist-em-all-ogee) or Theory of Knowledge: Philosophers are interested in how we learn and understand things. Sometimes they think about how our five senses work, and sometimes they think about ideas that pop into our heads without having to use our eyes and ears. They also like to think about the difference between things that are true, and things that are false.

Ethics (eth-icks) or Theory of Good and Bad: Philosophers think about the difference between doing the right thing and doing the wrong thing. This also leads them to think about what it means to live a good life, and be a good person.

Aesthetics (a-stet-icks) or Theory of Beauty: Philosophers wonder what makes something beautiful or ugly. They also love to think about the difference between great works of art, and big, ugly messes. This means exploring the reasons why we like some things and not others, and how artists come up with new and exciting pieces of work.

Politics: Philosophers discuss who should be in charge of everyone, how leaders should make decisions, and how groups of people can change the way they work together.

There are so many types of philosophy that we could fill a whole other book with them. Philosophers love to ask questions about just about any subject. There's philosophy of history, philosophy of science, philosophy of fluffy bunny slippers...